A DREAM and A DOLLAR

Strategies that will help you BREAK OUT of your "Dream Bubble"

RAY ORR

WHOLE ARMOUR PUBLISHING
WWW.wholearmourpublishing.com

A Dream and A Dollar
ISBN 0-9622860-2-8

Copyright © 2003 by Ray Orr
P. O. Box 223722
Dallas, Texas 75222-3722

Published by Whole Armour Publishing
P. O. Box 223722
Dallas, Texas 75222-3722
Printed in the United States of America.

Marilyn,
We did it! —
You're The Greatest.
Thanks for your
expertise + counsel.
Keep Dreaming!

A Dream and A Dollar was inspired by a true story.

My story!

Dedication

This book is dedicated to my lovely wife of twenty-two years, Patrice. Her steadfast belief and confidence in me are a constant source of strength. She is the love of my life: my soul mate, help-meet, friend, advisor, and sounding board. Thanks for supporting me and allowing me to pursue my dreams.

Next to God and oxygen, she is the most important thing in my life. We had a storybook beginning. I was at church one Sunday and the pastor asked for all of the singles in the church to stand. While standing, I looked around and when I saw her, I was captivated by her beauty and poise. I knew she was the one for me!

Contents

Acknowledgments

Ella Kuykendall, my mother who risked it all that I might live. Thanks for being a living example of faith, courage, and tenacity. Also, for mortgaging your house so I could pursue my dream.

In loving memory of my Aunt Mary and Uncle Joe Taylor who helped to raise me. I love you!

To my surviving big brothers, William Taylor, Johnnie Orr, and James Orr. I could not have made it without you.

My four children: Jacqueline, my firstborn; Andrea, Ray, Jr., and Reuben. Thanks for listening to my dreams over the years and for encouraging me and believing in me. Also, for helping to edit *A Dream and A Dollar.*

Christopher Howell, who is like a son to me. Thanks for having a listening ear and for all your contributions to *A Dream and A Dollar.*

Wanda Cook who invested her last $3 in my dream, and for calling and encouraging me over the years.

Harvey Miller, thanks for your support, time, and effort.

To Freddie Jones, my former growth group leader and a dear friend.

To you whom I have not named, please know that even though you are unnamed in this manuscript, you are not unknown to me. You are greatly appreciated!

Introduction

What's your dream? I believe there is a dream inside all of us. I believe that *A Dream and A Dollar* is your story and that is why you are reading this book. Most of us have more than a dollar. The phrase "a dollar" represents not having nearly enough money and capital to make your dream a reality. There are a few individuals who have millions and billions of dollars, but the vast majority of us have only "a dollar" (not nearly enough money).

While money is not everything, it takes money to pursue your dream. Zig Ziglar says, "Money isn't everything, but it's reasonably close to oxygen." I submit to you that money gives you options and privileges. The more money you have, the more options and privileges you have. Money is needed to make your dream a reality. Even if someone extends favor to you and says you don't have to pay for something, money is still involved. They are using their money and resources to finance your dream.

> Zig Ziglar says, "Money isn't everything, but it's reasonably close to oxygen."

On the front cover of this book is a man with a dream and a dollar. His dream is capsuled inside of a "dream bubble," and he has a dollar in his hand. Inside of his "dream bubble" is his family, career, nice home, luxury car – the American dream. By all accounts his dream is very modest. After all, living in America, the wealthiest country in the world, his dream should not be viewed as an unrealistic dream.

Personally, I can identify with the illustration on the front cover, because it is a page out of my own life. This book, *A Dream and A Dollar*, mirrors the average American. My mission in these pages is to share with you some proven and timeless strategies to help you break out of your dream bubble and realize your dream!

Dare To Dream

If you dare, you can make your dream a reality. And Ray Orr will show you how!

CHAPTER

Dare To Dream

I challenge you to "dare to dream." "Dare" means to be bold; to have enough courage or audacity for some act; to be fearless; to venture; to oppose and defy; to challenge (someone) to do something hard, dangerous, or rash, especially as a test of courage.[1]

After you have dared to dream, you must take a leap of faith. Taking a leap of faith requires taking action because **"faith without works is dead."** You have to dare to dream even when you have no way to manifest it. You have to move from being a dreamer to becoming a doer. You can't keep dreaming about a change. You have got to be willing to make a change and then do it: Make the change! You have to redirect your time, energy, money, resources, and capital.

You've got to get up early and stay up late. You've got to stop being a couch potato and a TV remote addict. You've got to make sacrifices. The bigger the dream, the bigger the cost. Are you willing to pay the cost of admission? Are you willing to pay the cost to realize your dream? It all

> You've got to stop being a couch potato and a TV remote addict.

[1] *Webster's New World College Dictionary*, Fourth Ed. (Foster City, CA: IDG Books Worldwide, Inc., 1999, 2002), 367.

comes down to how bad you want it. You have to take a risk and the greatest risk is not taking one!

I remember back in 1980 when I was working as a Senior Sales Representative with Federal Express Corporation in Dallas, Texas. I had a dream that I wanted to own my own business. I was like most Americans who wanted to own their own business, but I didn't know what kind of business I wanted to own. However, I knew I wanted it to be a service-oriented business that was mainstream and not limited to a certain zip code or geographical area of the country.

> I practiced and imitated business owners in how they stood, talked, and dressed, and I observed and imitated their overall demeanor.

I would spend two hours a day dreaming about owning my own business and two to four hours a day working on my dream. Even though I didn't know the specific kind of business I wanted to start, I started reading biographies and autobiographies of successful business owners and entrepreneurs. That was inspiring and motivational to me. I practiced and imitated business owners in how they stood, talked, and dressed, and I observed and imitated their overall demeanor.

I set up an office in my home, and I called it the Home Office/Corporate Office. I had a desk, chairs, phone, fax machine, filing cabinet – all the things I had at my office at FedEx. I would go in that office, put my feet up on my desk, and call my imaginary secretary into my office and go over my appointments for the day with her. I would call in my Vice President and give him directives and call in the Vice President of Sales and ask him how we were doing with our sales projections.

In my mind, I was running a major corporation out of my home office. Now, this was long ago before the "Home Office" or "Home-Based Business" concept was acceptable and widely in use. I was making preparations for my dream and calling the things that were not as though they were.

One day while I was still employed with FedEx, I was visiting with one of my customers who owned a commercial mailing service. I asked him what he did, and he offered to give me a tour of his facility. We went into the production area, and he showed me around. He showed me the inserting machine that would open an envelope, stuff up to five letters in it, put water on the envelope, and automatically seal it. I was fascinated with it, and it made my dream "leap."

There is a Bible story in the book of Luke about Mary, who was pregnant with Jesus. She went to visit her relative, Elizabeth, who was pregnant too. When Elizabeth heard the greeting of Mary, Elizabeth's baby leaped in her womb.

When the owner of that commercial mailing service identified his inserting machine and told me more about the mailing service, my dream leaped within me. I knew it was the business I wanted to go into. That day I saw my dream in a physical form, and I literally touched my dream.

Be Passionate!

Since that day in 1980, I became passionate about my dream. You have to be passionate about your dream, because passion will drive you. Men especially are driven by passion. From 1980 through 1983 I became preoccupied greatly with the mailing service business. I said to myself, "I will prepare and someday my chance will come."

Prepare!

I spent from 1980 through 1983 in market research and networking. I began to go to the library and read up on the mailing service industry.

A commercial mailer is a company that engages in the preparation of bulk quantities of mail for direct mail. This entails data processing, affixing labels to envelopes, inserting, folding, sorting, and custom handwork, plus fulfillment. I found out it was a $10 billion a year industry. Also, I found out that the commercial mailing service business was a "sleeper" to many – that is, a business that many people were unaware of.

I discovered that at that time there were only approximately twenty commercial mailers in the Dallas/Fort Worth metroplex and approximately 5,000 commercial mailers nationwide. I found out that the mailing service business was tough to break into and highly competitive. As a part of my preparation, I visited other commercial mailing service companies in Dallas and around the country.

I became acquainted with two commercial mailing service owners in the Dallas area who later became pivotal in the success of my dream. I met Dan Cowan, the owner of Total Marketing Company, and Helen Donnell, the owner of Ridgeway Mailing Service. Helen Donnell told me that Ridgeway Mailing Service was the first commercial mailing service in the metroplex.

My First Investor!

On August 1, 1982, while in a church service, Pastor Ross Cullins, the assistant pastor at the church I attended at that time, challenged the men in the church to get together, pool their resources, and start their own businesses. I knew that word was for me, so when he finished preaching, I went to the altar for prayer. I asked the pastor to pray that I would have wisdom to start my own business. The pastor prayed for me and I left the altar. As I was walking back to my seat, a lady, Wanda Cook, stopped me and told me she wanted to invest in my business. She told me she believed in me and knew I could do it.

Now, I didn't have a business at that time. It was only a dream, so actually she was investing in my dream. Wanda Cook gave me three $1 bills and told me that was all the money she had and she was giving it to me.

Wanda Cook became the first investor in my dream with her last three $1 bills. Her act warmed my heart immensely, because she was not an affluent woman. As a matter of fact, she didn't even have a job. Wanda was financially and economically challenged and appeared to be very limited in employment skills. I was tempted not to take her money, because I knew her plight. Plus, I had a very high-income job with FedEx, and my wife had a high-income job with Dial Corporation. Our cash flow was fluent.

I accepted Wanda's three $1 bills. I told her, "Thank you for your support and confidence in me." I kept those three $1 bills and looked at them almost every day. Her contribution inspired and motivated me to go on because of the confidence this single, challenged woman had in me and my dream. Those three $1 bills served as a constant reminder and motivational stimulus to me. Whenever I thought about giving up and abandoning my dream, I would look at those three $1 bills. They inspired, motivated, and encouraged me to keep pursuing my dream and to never give up!

Personal Responsibility

I soon realized that in order for this dream to become a reality, it needed full-time attention. I thought possibly I could hire someone else to start the business for me and I could keep my job at FedEx. After all, being a Senior Sales Rep with FedEx was a very prestigious and financially rewarding position. But that idea wasn't working, so it was time for me to take a leap of faith. I found out *it is your own responsibility to build your dream, not someone else's responsibility.*

All I had was a dream and a dollar, but never underestimate the power of a dream and a dollar!

I talked it over with my wife. I said, "In order for me to start this business and build it, I need to resign from FedEx and devote full time to making this dream a reality." She was in sales for Dial Corporation and made enough money to cover our monthly household expenses.

So on October 31, 1982, I dared to pursue my dream, took a leap of faith, and resigned from FedEx. All I had was a dream and a dollar, but never underestimate the power of *a dream and a dollar!*

Putting the Pedal to the Metal!

I went to the county clerk's office in downtown Dallas and got an assumed name and started operating out of my home as Orr Mailing Service.

> *I refused to let the opposition diminish my dream.*

I soon realized that I needed to be in a building and in a business district, so I put together my loan request proposal and drew up my business plan. Then I went to over twenty banks. Each bank officer complimented me on my professional proposal and business plan, but they would not loan me any money.

None of the banking officials were familiar with the commercial mailing service business and would not loan money on a high risk start-up business they weren't familiar with. These bank officers were gun-shy about new business start-ups. I even applied for a loan with the Small Business Administration (SBA), and they said, "No." I heard "no" so much that I got immune to "no." *But I refused to let the opposition diminish my dream.*

January 1983 marked four months since I had resigned from FedEx. The steady paychecks had ceased, and I had depleted all of my seed money that I had saved to birth my dream. When you don't have a steady paycheck coming in, your savings seem to take wings and fly away! My dream of owning my own business, of being wealthy and influential, was starting to look like a disaster and was becoming a nightmare. My dream had become a drain. I became scared, frustrated, aggravated, angry, exhausted, and disappointed, but still, *I refused to give up on my dream.*

One day my good friend and mentor, Freddie Jones, who knew my plight, told me he knew of a bank, Allied Lakewood Bank, where a colleague of his had gotten a loan. He said they appeared to be friendly toward start-up businesses.

OFFICE OF RICHARD COX , COUNTY CLERK, DALLAS COUNTY, TEXAS
500 MAIN STREET, DALLAS, TEXAS 75202

ASSUMED NAME RECORDS
CERTIFICATE OF OWNERSHIP FOR UNINCORPORATED BUSINESS OR PROFESSION

NOTICE: "CERTIFICATES OF OWNERSHIP" ARE VALID ONLY FOR A PERIOD NOT TO EXCEED 10 YEARS FROM THE DATE FILED
IN THE COUNTY CLERK'S OFFICE. (Chapter 36, Sect. 1, Title 4 — Business and Commerce Code)

(This certificate properly executed is to be filed immediately with the County Clerk)

* * * * * * *

NAME IN WHICH BUSINESS IS OR WILL BE CONDUCTED

Dare Mail... Ser...

BUSINESS ADDRESS P O Box 1.71

CITY: Dallas   STATE: T.x.   ZIP CODE: 75...7

PERIOD (not to exceed 10 years) DURING WHICH ASSUMED NAME WILL BE USED:

BUSINESS IS TO BE CONDUCTED AS (Check Which One): ☐ Proprietorship ☐ Sole Practitioner ☐ Joint Venture
☐ General Partnership ☐ Limited Partnership ☐ Real Estate Investment Trust
☐ Joint Stock Company ☐ Other (name type) _____

CERTIFICATE OF OWNERSHIP

I/We, the undersigned, are the owner_____ of the above business and my/our name_____ and address_____ given
is/are true and correct, and there is/are no ownership(s) in said business other than those listed herein below.

— NAMES OF OWNERS —

NAME RAY ORR   SIGNATURE Ray O

Address _____ Residence _____ Zip Code _____

NAME _____ (print or type) SIGNATURE _____

Address _____ Residence _____ Zip Code _____

NAME _____ (print or type) SIGNATURE _____

Address _____ Residence _____ Zip Code _____

NAME _____ (print or type) SIGNATURE _____

Address _____ Residence _____ Zip Code _____

NAME _____ (print or type) SIGNATURE _____

Address _____ Residence _____ Zip Code _____

THE STATE OF TEXAS |
                      |
COUNTY OF DALLAS |

BEFORE ME, THE UNDERSIGNED AUTHORITY, on this day personally appeared Ray Orr

known to me to be the person_____ whose name_____ is/are subscribed to the foregoing instrument and acknowledged to me
that_____ he_____ is/are the owner(s) of the above-named business and that_____ he_____ signed the same for the
purpose and consideration therein expressed.

GIVEN UNDER MY HAND AND SEAL OF OFFICE, on 11/15/   19 82

(SEAL)   RICHARD COX , COUNTY CLERK

                              By _____ Deputy
                              Bernice Conley

                              Notary Public in and for Dallas County, Texas

I went to this bank with my loan proposal and business plan. Since I didn't have the name of a particular loan officer, I just asked to see a loan officer. Rick Bridgewater, one of the loan officers, introduced himself to me. We went to his office where I made my presentation to him.

One of Rick's bank customers was the owner of a commercial mailing service, so he was familiar with the type of business and understood how it made money. Even though Rick was familiar with this type of business, he was reluctant to commit to making a loan to me, but he didn't say "no." The fact that he didn't say "no" was like saying sic 'em to a bulldog!

Over the next sixty days, I must have visited with Rick about thirty times. I began to appeal to the entrepreneurial spirit that was on the inside of him. (That same entrepreneurial spirit may be inside of you too!)

Finally, Rick began to believe in my dream and believe that I could make it a reality. Rick became a partner with me in the pursuit of my dream, not in a cash aspect, but as far as believing in me.

The old saying is true that persistence wears down resistance.

The old saying is true that *persistence wears down resistance.* Rick and I became friends, and we were on a first-name basis. He was very pointed with me and said the first thing I needed to do was to adjust the loan request amount in my proposal. My loan request was for $100,000.

On the pages that follow, I have included a copy of one of my loan request application letters and a Statement of Denial. I want you to know some of the challenges I went through to get my dream off the ground. I found out quickly that you've got to have a "no quit" mentality and a "never give up" attitude!

Raymond Orr

InterFirst Bank Dallas
P.O. Box 83132
Dallas, Texas 75283

Dear Gentlemen:

The purpose of this letter is to request a loan in the amount of
$100,000 in order to assist in the opening of Dallas Mailing
Service. The money will be used for equipment leasing and operating capital.

I would like to request that the company be given a term of five
years to repay the loan, preferably on a monthly installment
program.

I have had a professional business relationship with InterFirst
Bank management for the last four years. Enclosed is a loan proposal.

Respectfully,

Raymond Orr

Enclosures

Raymond Orr

November 23, 1982

Mr. Costa Mitchakes
RepublicBank Dallas
P.O. Box 225961
Dallas, Texas   75265

Dear Mr. Mitchakes:

The purpose of this letter is to request a loan in the amount of
$100,000 in order to assist in the opening of Orr Mailing Service.
The money will be used for equipment leasing and operating capital.

I would like to request that the company be given a term of five
years to repay the loan, preferably on a monthly installment program
with a six months reprieval.

I have had a professional business relationship with RepublicBank
management for the last four years. I currently have a saving account
and business account with your institution. Enclosed is a loan
proposal.

Sincerely,

Ray Orr

Enclosures

STATEMENT OF CREDIT DENIAL, TERMINATION, OR CHANGE
FOR NATIONAL BANKS

DATE 12-9-82

DESCRIPTION OF ACCOUNT, TRANSACTION, OR REQUESTED CREDIT

| $100,000.00 | 90 Days | To operate Orr Mailing Service New Co. |

DESCRIPTION OF ADVERSE ACTION TAKEN

Raymond Orr

Loan request denied

PRINCIPAL REASON(S) FOR ADVERSE ACTION CONCERNING CREDIT

- ☐ Credit application incomplete
- ☐ Insufficient credit references
- ☐ Unable to verify credit references
- ☐ Temporary or irregular employment
- ☐ Unable to verify employment
- ☐ Length of employment
- ☐ Insufficient income
- ☐ Excessive obligations
- ☐ Unable to verify income
- ☒ Inadequate collateral
- ☐ Too short a period of residence

- ☐ Temporary residence
- ☐ Unable to verify residence
- ☐ No credit file
- ☐ Insufficient credit file
- ☐ Delinquent credit obligations
- ☐ Garnishment, attachment, foreclosure, repossession, or suit
- ☐ Bankruptcy
- ☐ We do not grant credit to any applicant on the terms and conditions you request.
- ☐ Other, specify _____

DISCLOSURE OF USE OF INFORMATION OBTAINED FROM AN OUTSIDE SOURCE

☒ Disclosure inapplicable

☐ Information obtained in a report from a consumer reporting agency

NAME

STREET ADDRESS   PHONE

☐ Information obtained from an outside source other than a consumer reporting agency. Under the Fair Credit Reporting Act, you have the right to make a written request, within 60 days of receipt of this notice, for disclosure of the nature of the adverse information.

Republic National Bank of Dallas
CREDITOR'S NAME

Pacific and Ervay Streets, Dallas, Texas 75201
CREDITOR'S ADDRESS

CREDITOR'S PHONE 653-5758

EQUAL CREDIT OPPORTUNITY ACT NOTICE

The Federal Equal Credit Opportunity Act prohibits creditors from discriminating against credit applicants on the basis of race, color, religion, national origin, sex, marital status, age (provided that the applicant has the capacity to enter into a binding contract); because all or part of the applicant's income derives from any public assistance program; or because the applicant has in good faith exercised any right under the Consumer Credit Protection Act. The Federal agency that administers compliance with this law concerning this creditor is Comptroller of the Currency, Consumer Affairs Division, Washington, D. C. 20219.

Republic National Bank of Dallas   (Creditor)

HPT 350-0005/26

Let me give you a clear picture of exactly where I was. I wanted the bank to loan me $100,000 for a start-up business. I was twenty-nine years old with no prior experience in the mailing service business, and I had no assets and no collateral. Obviously, I had no way to guarantee the bank that they could recoup their money if my dream failed. Rick explained to me why I kept getting a "no" from the banks. Both he and I knew it was a long shot for me to get financing from his bank.

In a way, I was like an underdog. However, many people love to pull for the underdog. That's the person or team least likely to win. Rick genuinely wanted to see this business venture launched. Anytime I called his office to talk with him, he always welcomed my calls and was glad to hear from me. Rick made it very clear, however, that if I didn't have some sort of collateral, I would not get a loan from his bank. I soon learned that *banks do not loan money on dreams!* They loan money on the basis of assets and collateral.

A Financial Strategy

Rick and I came up with a strategy for financing my dream. The strategy was that if I bought a $10,000 certificate of deposit with his bank, then the bank would loan me $20,000. That was a great strategy, but I didn't have $10,000. As a matter of fact, I didn't even have $100. As you can see, all I had was *a dream and a dollar!* Rick said it was doubtful that any other bank or financial institution would make such a similar generous deal to an unproven start-up company run by a twenty-nine year old with limited business ownership and entrepreneurial experience.

Put Feet to What You Believe

I kept telling myself, "While I'm waiting on my breakthrough, I will prepare and someday my chance will come." So I started looking for a building. I learned that most of the commercial mailing service companies were located in the Dallas Market Center District near downtown Dallas. I began looking for a building in that area, and I met a real estate agent, Bob Darrouzet.

I told Bob I was interested in a building in that area and I would be moving in a few months. Bob showed me a 7,200 square-foot building on Levee Street, which had a breath-taking, panoramic view of the Dallas downtown skyline. It was love at first sight. I told Bob this was the building I wanted. Remember, though, at this point all I had was *a dream and a dollar!*

Even though you may have only *a dream and a dollar,* you can't just sit around wishing and waiting. Keep working as you wait so when the door of opportunity opens, you are ready to run through it.

Big "D" Mailing Service, Inc.

While I was in the waiting process, I decided to change the name of the company. I wanted a name that tied in with the Dallas image – I can!, ethical, efficient, affluent, cosmopolitan, and progressive. So I began to brainstorm and I chose the name, Dallas Mailing Service, but that name was already taken. So I went back to my brain-storming closet. At this time, the slang for Dallas was Big "D." So I decided to name the company, *Big "D" Mailing Service.*

Preparation precedes possession.

I sincerely believe that *preparation pre-cedes possession.* I can't overemphasize the importance of preparation and being ready for the next step. It may seem like a waste of time, but it is not.

Financial Breakthrough

One day I was talking with my mother who lived in Memphis, sharing my financial challenge with her. She said, "Remember the house I own in Mississippi that I have rented out and you are managing for me? Why don't you sell it because I am going to leave it for you anyway?"

I made an offer to the tenant in the house, and he agreed to buy the house. The proceeds that I cleared from the sale of the house totaled $3,333. Needless to say, the proceeds from the sale of the house in Mississippi were way short of the $10,000 I needed. So I went back to the strategy room!

During this time I was listening to tapes and reading books about successful individuals. I was reading *Absolutely Positively Overnight,* which is a story about the first ten years of the Federal Express Corporation and its commanding general, Memphian Fred Smith. I could identify because I had been employed with FedEx and was from Memphis.

I remember reading that his personal seed money was not enough to launch his venture, so he had to get some investors. So my next strategy was to get some investors. I remembered my assistant pastor's challenge so I got two friends from church who were already full-time business owners. Each invested $3,333.33 and together we came up with $10,000.

On Friday, February 25, 1983, at 11:30 a.m., the investors and I met with Rick at Allied Lakewood Bank and purchased a $10,000 certificate of deposit, and the bank loaned me $20,000. Now I had my seed capital and operating capital.

Major Breakthrough!

It was on March 1, 1983, that I renamed Orr Mailing Service to Big "D" Mailing Service, Inc. I moved into a commercial building in the Industrial Business Park near the Dallas Market Center.

In October 2002, we celebrated twenty years of business. My company has been the recipient of numerous prestigious business awards. I have been featured in numerous national magazines and newspapers, and I have been selected as the Entrepreneur of the Week by the *Dallas Morning Newspaper.* This was a very special honor to me, considering that Dallas is the hub of some of the nation's top entrepreneurs.

I dared to dream and succeeded against all odds. You have to dream too, for your dream will fuel you and give you energy, inspiration, and motivation. A dream will give you a sense of where you want to go. It is a picture of a desirable future. The future is made up of dreams. Thousands of movements, revolutions, organizations, and corporations have been started because of a dream.

> You have to dream too, for your dream will fuel you and give you energy, inspiration, and motivation.

In the next chapter we will look at a few other individuals who dared to dream. Each of these people took a leap of faith, and today they are enshrined in the "Dare To Dream" Hall of Fame!

"Dare To Dream"
Hall of Famers!

FOLLOW YOUR DREAM

Follow your dream . . .
Take one step at a time,
And don't settle for less,
Just continue to climb.

Follow your dream . . .
If you stumble, don't stop
And lose sight of your goal.
Press on to the top.

For only on top
Can we see the whole view,
Can we see what we've done
And what we can do.

Can we then have the vision
To seek something new . . .
Press on,
And follow your dream.

Amanda Bradley

CHAPTER 2

"Dare To Dream"
Hall of Famers!

I n this chapter, we'll look at a few ordinary people who dared to dream, took leaps of faith, and either have or are yet accomplishing extraordinary feats.

The Reverend Dr. Martin Luther King, Jr.

The Reverend Dr. Martin Luther King, Jr. dared to dream. Dr. King coined the phrase, "I have a dream." Dr. King's, "I have a dream," stirred our entire nation as well as the whole world. His dream captured the imagination of our nation. "I have a dream" started a whole movement. This man dared to dream. One man with a dream changed the course of history. There is power in a dream!

The Biographical Outline of Dr. King says:

Dr. King's concept of "somebodies," which symbolized the celebration of human worth and the conquest of subjugation, gave black and poor people hope and a sense of dignity. His philosophy of nonviolent direct action, and his strategies for rational and non-destructive social change, galvanized the conscience of this nation and reordered its priorities. His wisdom, his work, his actions, his commitment, and his dream for a new way of life are intertwined with the American experience.[2]

Dr. King was passionate about his dream. You must be passionate about your dream too. Men especially are driven with passion. Dr. Martin Luther King, Jr. was a man of great conviction, and he was committed to his dream. He died while pursuing his dream. In fact, his dream cost him his life. He was assassinated on April 4, 1968.

Your dream will cost you something too. How far are you willing to follow your dream?

Martin Luther King, Jr. and "I have a dream" became synonymous. His dream and his unflinching character have been inspirational to all of us.

Dr. King said, "I have a dream that one day . . . the sons of former slave-owners will be able to sit down together at the table of brotherhood . . . I have a dream that my four children will one day live in a nation where they will not be judged by the color of their skin, but by the content of their character."[3]

In his sermon, "I've Been to the Mountaintop," given on April 3, 1968, Dr. King said, "Let us rise up tonight with a greater readiness. Let us stand with a greater determination. And let us move on in these powerful days, these days of challenge to make America what it ought to be. We have an opportunity to make America a better nation. . . ."[4]

After mentioning the death threats that were on his life, Dr. King said:

> Well, I don't know what will happen now. We've got some difficult days ahead. But it really doesn't matter with me now, because I've been to the mountaintop and I don't

[2]"Biographical Outline of Dr. Martin Luther King, Jr.," http://www.thekingcenter.org/mlk/biolhtml, Accessed December 11, 2002.
[3]From an August 28, 1963, speech in Washington, DC.
[4]http://www.thekingcenter.org/mlk/bio.html, Accessed December 11, 2002.

mind. Like anybody, I would like to live a long life. Longevity has its place. But I'm not concerned about that now. I just want to do God's will, and He's allowed me to go up to the mountain. And I've looked over and I've seen the Promised Land. I may not get there with you, but I want you to know tonight, that we as a people will get to the Promised Land. And I'm happy tonight; I'm not worried about anything. I'm not fearing any man. Mine eyes have seen the glory of the coming of the Lord.[5]

> Take a leap of faith and use what you have to get your dream moving!

Dr. King's dream fueled a revolution. There was mighty power in his dream, just as there is in your dream. Take a leap of faith and use what you have to get your dream moving!

Dr. King earned a B.A. degree in Sociology from Morehouse College in 1948. He received a Bachelor of Divinity Degree from Crozer Theological Seminary in 1951. Then he pursued doctoral studies at Boston University later in 1951 and earned a Ph.D. degree in 1955. He also studied at Harvard University. "Dr. King was awarded honorary degrees from various colleges and universities in the United States and several foreign countries . . . Dr. King received numerous awards for his leadership in the Civil Rights Movement."[6]

Mary Kay Ash

Mary Kay Ash, the founder of Mary Kay Cosmetics, dared to dream. At a very young age, this future author of three best-sellers was already building a foundation for belief in herself. She grew up in Hot Wells, Texas, as Mary Kathlyn Wagner.

At age six, she cared for her seriously ill father while her mother worked fourteen hours a day in a Houston restaurant. Mary Kay cooked, cleaned, brought home straight A report cards, took trophies in typing and debate, and outsold every other Girl Scout sell-

[5]Ibid.
[6]Ibid.

> "My mother's words became the theme of my childhood . . . they have stayed with me all my life: 'You can do it!'"

ing cookies and in ticket sales for other school events. She said, "My mother's words became the theme of my childhood . . . they have stayed with me all my life: 'You can do it!'"

After twenty-five years as a record-breaking sales person, Mary Kay Ash launched her own company, primarily to give other women what she had lacked on the job: motivation, recognition, and empowerment. She said, "My objective was to give women the opportunity to do anything they were smart enough to do."

The launch of Ash's cosmetic company was hindered with her husband's death just one month before the scheduled opening. But strengthened by the encouragement of her two sons and daughter, Mary Kay formally launched her company on Friday, September 13, 1963.

There will be many challenges and distractions on your road to seeing your dream become a reality, but you must embrace the moment and fearlessly work toward the manifestation of it. Despite the obstacles, Mary Kay was determined to see her dream come true not only for her and her three children, but for the hundreds of thousands of women and men who would be inspired by her strength and tenaciousness.

Mary Kay, Inc. is the largest direct seller of skin care products in the United States. The 1999 global wholesale sales topped the $1 billion mark. The company's independent sales force is more than 900,000 strong, operating in thirty-five countries worldwide.

The company's 38th annual convention meeting, held in Dallas, Texas, on Thursday, July 18, 2002, through Saturday, August 3, 2002, was attended by approximately 50,000 Sales Reps.[7]

---

[7]The Dallas Morning News, July 18, 2002.

Because Mary Kay Ash dared to dream, her cosmetics company became a reality, and she has enriched the lives of women all over the world.

What's your dream? Do you have a theme or a phrase to drive you to press ahead during difficult times?

Frederick W. Smith

Fred Smith, founder and CEO of Federal Express Corporation, dared to dream. His dream of three decades ago absolutely, positively caused a revolution! His dream changed how man communicates. In 1971 when Frederick W. Smith founded Federal Express Corporation, he was twenty-seven years old.

When Fred Smith put his concept on paper, it was average. When he moved on this idea and made it a reality, it was a struggle. And when he guaranteed delivery of a package by 10:30 a.m., the name "Federal Express" became part of America's culture.

While attending Yale University in the mid 1960's, Smith submitted a term paper detailing the hub-and-spoke process that would become the core of Federal Express Corporation. His grade, a "C." An average mark for a man who would prove to be so exceptional!

Before he turned his term paper into a multi-billion dollar giant, Fred Smith served as a Marine in Vietnam. He experienced some of the worst fighting in the war and after two tours of duty, he returned home with captain's bars, a chest full of medals (Silver Star, Bronze Star, two Purple Hearts, Presidential Regiment Citation), and life experiences not taught in a Yale classroom.

When he returned home, Smith took control of Arkansas Aviation Sales, an ailing business in which his family held interest. Smith saw little future for a company selling aviation gas and offering hangar services, so he began searching for new markets and found one in supplying parts for the emerging corporate jet market. The company prospered in its new mission, but Smith faced one major headache: frequent delays in receiving "rush" repair parts.

Believing he was not alone with this challenge, Smith saw a number of opportunities for the use of express air delivery and developed the notion that this service could thrive in a United States economy that was becoming service-oriented.

In 1971, Fred Smith purchased two Falcon airplanes and incorporated Federal Express. He funded his dream with $8 million of family money, $40 million from investors, and $90 million in bank financing. Federal Express became the largest start-up company ever funded by venture capital at that time.

In 1973, FedEx began service by offering overnight, second day, and $5 Courier Pack services to twenty-five cities. On its first night of operation, Federal Express processed six packages, one being a bag of dirty laundry from a FedEx salesman. But Smith pressed on, and by the year's end Federal Express was serving forty cities and owned thirty-three airplanes.

Developments within competitive businesses during the early 1970's gave Federal Express a boost. Air passenger traffic grew rapidly, causing passengers' luggage to replace shippers' parcels. Competitor REA Express went bankrupt. In 1974, United Parcel Service (UPS) union employees went on strike.

By 1975 FedEx showed a profit of $175,000. Today the company shows an annual gross income of $20 billion. All because one man, Frederick W. Smith, with one dream, caused a business revolution!

Oprah Winfrey

A precocious child, Winfrey often performed in public from an early age. Her unruly behavior led her mother to send her from their Milwaukee, Wisconsin, home to live in Nashville, Tennessee, with her father, who proved to be a guiding influence on her life.

Winfrey majored in speech and drama at Tennessee State University, and as a freshman she was selected Miss Tennessee. Oprah began her broadcasting career at WVOL radio in Nashville while still in high school. At the age of nineteen, she became the youngest person and the first African-American woman to anchor the news at Nashville's WTVF-TV. She then moved to Baltimore's WJZ-TV to co-anchor the six o'clock news and moved on to become co-host of their local talk show, "People Are Talking."

In 1984, Oprah moved to Chicago to host WLS-TV's morning talk show, "A.M. Chicago," which became the number one talk show just one month after she began. In less than a year, the show expanded to one hour and was renamed "The Oprah Winfrey Show." In 1986, "The Oprah Winfrey Show" entered national syndication and has remained the number one talk show for the last seventeen consecutive seasons, receiving thirty-five Emmy Awards. Oprah produces and hosts "The Oprah Winfrey Show" through Harpo Productions. It is seen by 26 million viewers a week in the United States, it is broadcast in 106 countries, and it is the highest-rated talk show in television history.

> "The Oprah Winfrey Show" entered national syndication and has remained the number one talk show for the last seventeen consecutive seasons.

Oprah, with an even bigger dream, broadened her scope into other areas in addition to being a successful talk show host and producer. She has become a magazine founder and editorial director; the founder of Oxygen Media, a women's cable network; and an educator in September 1999 when she joined Stedman Graham as an adjunct professor to co-teach "Dynamics of Leadership" at the J. L. Kellogg Graduate School of Management at Northwestern University.

Oprah Winfrey has inspired millions of people because of one dream!

Dave Thomas

Dave Thomas, founder of Wendy's, has been referred to by some people as "the accidental celebrity"! Dave always had a desire to own a restaurant. He started on this path at the age of twelve when he got his first restaurant job as a counterman in Knoxville, Tennessee.

In 1956, Dave Thomas was working at a barbecue restaurant in Fort Wayne, Indiana, when Colonel Harland Sanders of Kentucky Fried Chicken stopped in on a professional tour. Thomas's boss bought a KFC franchise, and six years later, Thomas went to Columbus to take over four failing Kentucky Fried Chicken restaurants. He sold them back to the founder in 1968 for $1.5 million, making him a millionaire at the age of thirty-five.

Thomas opened his first Wendy's Old-Fashioned Hamburgers in Columbus a year later. He named the restaurant after his eight-year-old daughter Melinda Lou, nicknamed Wendy by her siblings. Thomas said his burgers were square because Wendy's didn't cut corners.

Most fascinating is that Thomas thought he would be lucky to have three or four restaurants in Columbus. Today the Columbus phone book lists seventy-six Wendy's, with over 5,000 Wendy's restaurants worldwide. Thomas's understated "aw-shucks" style carried over from his real life to his books to his Wendy's TV ads.

> Dave Thomas's life from a "down-to-earth, lovable guy" serves as an inspiring success story to multitudes of people.

The fact that an average, adopted child who dropped out of high school could reach such a level of success should be an inspiration to anyone. Dave Thomas's life from a "down-to-earth, lovable guy" serves as an inspiring success story to multitudes of people.

Dave Thomas used his good fortune to help as many people as he could. He once said, "If I can get just one child a home, it would be better than selling a million hamburgers." Dave accomplished both many times over. Local agencies that provide help to children reported that Dave would just "drop in" from time to time to see how he could assist them.

Dave Thomas saw his dream become a reality. Your dream can become a reality too!

Debbi Fields

Debbi Fields, founder of Mrs. Fields' cookies, dared to dream! From a single retail shop in Northern California to worldwide recognition, Mrs. Fields' story is one of true American success.

As a young mother with no business experience, Mrs. Fields began in 1977. There were people who were quick to tell Debbi that she was crazy because "no business could survive just selling cookies."[8]

The qualities that played major roles in Debbi Fields' success were headstrong determination, a dynamic personality, and a sincere concern for people. Her mission has always been to create the highest quality product possible.[9]

The Fields' product packaging states:

> She has captured the hearts and taste buds of cookie eaters with her totally irresistible cookies! A secret recipe full of premium ingredients and custom-blend chocolates creates moist, unique, 100 percent indulgent cookies! Now you can treat yourself and your family to the fresh-baked goodness of Mrs. Fields' cookies at home.[10]

What makes Debbi Fields a "Dare to Dream" Hall of Famer? She says, "The important thing is not being afraid to take a chance. Remember, the greatest failure is to not try. Once you find something you love to do, be the best at doing it."[11]

* * *

Because these ordinary people, and others like them, were willing to risk everything to press toward their dreams, either they have

---

[8]www.mrsfields.com, Accessed December 24, 2002.
[9]Ibid.
[10]Ibid.
[11]Ibid.

You
can dare
to dream too,
and make
a difference
in many
people's
lives.

accomplished or presently are accomplishing extraordinary feats that have made the world a better place in which to live. You can dare to dream too, and make a difference in many people's lives.

A Dream or a Fantasy?

The Ten Dreamments

Thou shalt flee from dream haters.
Thou shalt not let other people define your dream.
Thou shalt not live out someone else's dream.
Thou shalt not covet thy neighbor's dream.
Thou shalt dream thy own dream.
Thou shalt dream like a fool.
Thou shalt dream daily.
Thou shalt work on your dream daily.
Thou shalt have a strategy for your dream.
Thou shalt network your dream.

Ray Orr

A Dream or a Fantasy?

I s what you have a dream, or is it a fantasy? You must be able to distinguish between a dream and a fantasy. *Webster's Dictionary* defines "dream" as a sequence of sensations, images, thoughts, etc. passing through a person's mind.[12] *Webster's Dictionary* defines "fantasy" as imagination or fancy, esp. wild, visionary fancy; a bizarre mental image; illusions; an odd notion; whim.[13]

Here are three examples of a fantasy to help you differentiate between a dream and a fantasy:

1. You want to be a center in the National Basketball Association (NBA). You are 5'10" tall, you weigh 250 lbs., you are forty years old, and your breakfast consists of milk and twinkies! Fantasy!

2. You apply for a position as a commercial airline pilot and you have never flown a plane before. You have not been to pilot school, and your only previous experience is piloting a plane on your PC. Fantasy!

---

[12]Webster's New World College Dictionary, Fourth Ed., 434.
[13]Ibid., 514.

3. You want to be the President of the United States of America. You are sixty-five years old, you are in bad health, you have no political experience, and you have a checkered past. Fantasy!

I think you get the picture! Let that dream die and dream again! There are times when you have to let a dream die and dream another dream. However, I would be remiss if I didn't tell you that oftentimes there is only one degree of separation between a dream and a fantasy. Dreams are intuitive. In other words, they are not easily rationalized. Many times it is not as black and white as the illustrations given previously.

There are times you may have a "pipe dream," which is a fantastic idea or a vain hope or plan. (Similar to hallucinations experienced by opium smokers!)

You need to have your own dream, not that of another person, such as your mother or father. It cannot be your spouse's dream. It must be your own dream.

Many people fail because they have the wrong dream. Parents sometimes put their "dream" or "aspirations" upon their children to become doctors, lawyers, preachers, teachers, or professional athletes. Those are good dreams, but they are not necessarily the child's dream.

Once you have qualified the dream and established that it is your dream and that it is a dream and not a fantasy, you can begin your journey from dream to reality.

Building Your Dream

Dream Seeds for Success

- Dreams are the seed for success.
- Dreams are the substance of every great achievement in life.
- Dreaming without doing is folly.
- Doing what you dream is wise.
- A dream without works will never become more than a wish.
- Anyone can dream, but doers make their dream a reality.
- Dreams without goals are like cars without gas. They go nowhere.
- To do big things, you have to dream BIG!
- It is not a calamity to die with your dreams unfulfilled, but it is a calamity not to dream.

CHAPTER 4

Building Your Dream

O nce you have established that you have a dream and not a fantasy, now you can start building. In between the dream and reality is what we call "the building process." The building process is what most people want to avoid. Building your dream is like building a house. You need a blueprint. It will take work.

> Building your dream is like building a house. You need a blueprint.

You have to build your dream, and it is your responsibility to build it. No dream will build itself or become a reality by itself. You have a physical responsibility to participate in the building of your dream. It doesn't just happen. You have to make it happen. Remember, dreaming without doing is fantasizing. If you think there is no effort required on your part, you're living in fantasy land!

Make It Happen!

Have you heard of the Big Bang Theory relating to dreams? You dream and bang, it happens! I don't think so! You have a human responsibility to help manifest your dream. *You can't expect to lie down a blunder and wake up a wonder!* You dream it! You build it! You have to work at it. You have to invest in your dream.

> You have a human responsibility to help manifest your dream. You can't expect to lie down a blunder and wake up a wonder!

There was a popular song years ago titled, "Let It Be Me." I submit to you, it takes more than dreaming or saying, "Let it be me!" You have to make it happen. Stop wishing and waiting and make it happen. Some people are "king" of wishful thinking. There's an old saying, "How do you get to Carnegie Hall?" Practice! Practice! Practice! How do you reach your dream? Build! Build! Build!

Develop Your Strategy

You need a building blueprint for getting from dream to reality. A building blueprint will tell you how to get from dream to reality. It will tell you how to build a house. Instead of calling it a blueprint, I will refer to it as a "strategy" – how to build your dream strategy. *Webster's Dictionary* defines "strategy" as the science of planning and directing large-scale military operations; a plan or action based on this; skill in managing or planning; a plan of action.[14]

You have to have a strategy. If you want your dream to become a reality, you need this formula:

Formula: Desire ☐ Strategy ☐ Reality

> You have to have a strategy. If you want your dream to become a reality, you need this formula: Formula: Desire + Strategy = Reality.

Desire. You have to want to see a manifestation of your dream bad enough. You have to think about it all the time and talk about it all the time. You have to be consumed with your dream. "Desire" means to wish or long for; crave; covet; a strong wish or craving.[15]

A few years after I started my business, Ed Bailey, a college friend, was in Dallas on a business trip, and we got together for lunch. He told me, "I knew you were going to start your own

[14]Ibid., 1416.
[15]Ibid., 391.

business one day, because I remember when we were in college and working together at the Post Office during the Christmas holidays. When you picked me up each morning all you talked about was starting your own business." You have to desire your dream to come into reality.

Desire is a powerful weapon. If you desire your dream bad enough, then you will make the necessary sacrifices to achieve whatever it is. The question is, how bad do you want it? I was willing to give up a steady paycheck and lose everything I had to start my own business and make my dream become a reality.

> If you desire your dream bad enough, then you will make the necessary sacrifices to achieve whatever it is.

Be Diligent

You've got to be diligent. You have to be dreaming and doing, not wishing and waiting. I believe you should spend at least two hours a day just dreaming about your dream. You'll have to get up early and stay up late. You'll have to throw yourself into your dream. Immerse yourself into it. You have to be totally convinced of the necessity for your dream to become a reality. It will be hard to get others to help you if they see or sense that you are not fully persuaded that it can happen.

The desire has to be so strong that it functions as your faith. You have to have hunger, convictions, seriousness, devotion, and commitment. You have to be smart, alert, and determined.

Action Steps

Here are seven action steps for making your dream a reality:

Step 1 - *Start!* Start where you are. You can go anyplace in the world from a starting place. You have to *start*. You have to push off from the shore. You have to *try*. You have to have action. Remember, **"Faith without works is dead."**

> You have to push off from the shore.

Don't confuse activity with accomplishment. When you are building your dream, you need momentum. You need to have movement. You've got to keep the momentum going (the big "M"). I'm the kind of person who, when I start something, then stop, I have to get remotivated all over again. That's why I try so hard not to stop.

It's like if you have a habit of going to the gym and working out each day, if you miss one day it is hard to go back the next day. It's even harder if you miss two days. It's the same way with building your dream. You should work on your dream every day. Make progress every day. Once you get started, keep working on it. If you stop, it is hard to get back in the flow and regain your momentum.

Years ago there was a song with the words, "Like a snowball rolling down the side of a hill, it's growing." You may not be able to see it, but your dream is growing. Take your time, baby! Walk, don't run. Take baby steps. It is a step-by-step process. Steady growth. Controlled growth. Manageable growth. It is exciting to watch your dream take form and grow.

> You will have to get out of your comfort zone. Your dream will stretch you. You will get stretch marks.

Step 2 - *Change! Change! Change!* Be open to change. See change as your friend and welcome it. Embrace it. A stubborn man will always be an ignorant man. Building your dream will change you. Building your dream will transform you. Building your dream will make you and your life uncomfortable. You will have to get out of your comfort zone. Your dream will stretch you. You will get stretch marks. I have plenty of stretch marks!

Remember, you are giving birth to something. Expect to be stretched. It's okay! Having a dream and giving birth to your dream will stretch you. You will be expanded and enlarged. Personally, I have been expanded and stretched. I have plenty of stretch marks and scars. But the joy and fulfillment that you receive from the birth of your dream cause the stretch marks and scars to become very insignificant.

Step 3 - *Write it down!* Write down your dream and be as specific as possible. Writing the dream down makes it clear and easier to communicate with others who may be able to help you. You can articulate the dream better when it is written down. Articulating the dream is key. Make it plain. There is just something about seeing your dream in print and being able to look at it during the day and at night. Put it by your headstand in your bedroom. Write it and put it on your bathroom mirror, in your car, and in other visual locations.

Step 4 - *Set some specific goals with time lines for reaching your dream.* You must set some goals, for the goals are steps and aims to achieving your dream. You may have to revise your goals from time to time and set new time lines. This will keep you from getting lax or becoming a slacker. Keep the pressure on yourself. Without pressure, most people will not perform to their optimal level. I recommend that you break your goals up into short-term, immediate, and long-term goals.

> Break your goals up into short-term, immediate, and long-term goals.

Step 5 - *Study, preparation, and hard work are essential.* Sometimes it may seem like preparation is a waste of time, but it is not. Athletes have training camps, which is a time of intense preparation. It's the time they get ready for the season ahead.

Research and study your field of endeavor. If your dream is to become a great singer, research great singers, study them, and read their biographies. Learn how they accomplished their dreams and what they went through to accomplish them. Commit yourself to your dream. Research is so important, because it will help you make informed decisions about your dream. I have a saying, "I will prepare, and someday my chance will come."

Develop your gifts and skills. Hone your gifts and skills and fine-tune them. You are the only person who can use your ability. It is an awesome responsibility. You have to master your craft and be passionate about mastering it. Become an expert in your field. Meditate and study. Always keep pen and paper handy to jot down thoughts and ideas.

Step 6 - *Marketing/sales strategy.* When I opened my business, I realized that I needed customers to put my dream into action. My mailing colleague, Dan Cowan, owner of Total Marketing, with whom I had been networking, embraced me and for the first three months, he kept giving me his overflow and farmed jobs out to me. Helen Donnell, owner of Ridgeway Mailing Service, counseled me on the mailing services and on how to quote jobs. It was wonderful that they farmed jobs out to me, but I had to come up with a strategy to get my own customers.

Since I didn't have a track record or name identification, my strategy was to sell price and faster turnaround on processing jobs. So I had to undercut the other mailing companies. I had some business cards printed with the slogan, "We have got the price to get your business and the service to keep it." That became my selling strategy. It worked!

I ran an ad in the yellow pages in red. I had to get the phone ringing. I had to generate traffic. I joined the Dallas Chamber of Commerce, the North Dallas Chamber of Commerce, the Christian Chamber of Commerce, and the Black Chamber of Commerce. I went to all of the conventions that came to town. Anyplace there was a large gathering of people, I was there passing out business cards and brochures. I purchased a mailing list of companies with annual sales of $250,000, and I did a mass mailing to them.

I had to create a "marketing machine." You have to market your dream and brand it, and sometimes you have to rebrand it. Package your dream. Plan. Research. Find a strategy or a formula that will work and keep working it.

You have to develop a budget for your dream. Your dream is like a new baby; it will cost you plenty of money and require plenty of your time.

> You have to market your dream and brand it, and sometimes you have to rebrand it.

Step 7 - *Keep building*. Keep on building. Your friends may be few, but keep on building in the midst of scoffers, hecklers, and cynical people. In the Bible, Noah kept on building the ark. Most people did not believe Noah when he told them a flood was coming, but he kept on building. You have to keep building. While you are building your dream, you can't run around telling everyone about your dream, because there are some dream killers.

Joseph in the Bible experienced dream killers – his own brothers! They attempted to kill him and his dream. You need discernment, because you will need people to help you build your dream. Not everyone will be happy for you.

Don't let people "bash" your dream. People mocked and laughed at Noah, but he kept on building. One day when the flood came, the same folks who had mocked and laughed at him wanted Noah to share his dream with them, but it was too late.

> People used to call me "a dreamer," but now they call me "an entrepreneur."

It is amazing how people will want to celebrate you and honor you after your dream becomes a reality. Many people told me I couldn't do it. They told me it was the wrong timing. They told me I needed to wait until we got another President in the White House, but I kept right on building. They used to call me "a dreamer," but now they call me "an entrepreneur." The same people who weren't with me in the beginning now want to share in my dream and in my success. But just as it was with Noah, it's too late.

Stay Motivated and Optimistic

Motivation is a key. You must stay motivated. You've got to be optimistic. You can't be pessimistic and expect people to support and follow you. Don't get stuck in a stage. You can't stop the ages and stages of life. You have to learn how to flow with them. You must continue to build your dream in the midst of your challenges; i.e., family, cash flow, health, etc.

Even though you may need to put your dream on a temporary hold, keep on building. Perhaps the timing isn't right; your family is not ready; or you have five or six little ones at home. Keep building. Keep researching. Build relationships. Network! Network! Network!

Be willing to streamline, modify, or scale back on your dream if necessary. Adjust it. Delay it. Maybe you need to get some help to make your dream a reality.

Nurture Your Dream

Listen to motivational tapes. Go to educational seminars or industry gatherings. Rome wasn't built in a day. The ark wasn't built in a day. How do you eat an elephant? One bite at a time!

Although your dream may be different than mine, whatever your dream is, you have to develop a strategy and build a structure for it. You have to plan and strategize on how to make it happen. You have to nurture your dream.

> You have to nurture your dream.

As a word of caution, there is a time and a place for everything. There is a "dream" time and a "do" time. A time to dream and a time to work. I believe you should spend at least two hours a day just dreaming about your dream and two to four hours a day working on your dream. However, if you are the primary income provider for your family, you may not be able to allocate that much time.

Do not quit your job if that is your only steady source of income. While you are building your dream, continue to work and dream. Here's a wakeup call for you: *Dreams don't pay the bills!* You've got to deal with reality. But keep working and keep dreaming. The mortgage company, the telephone company, and the utility companies don't want to hear that your dream is going to make it big "one day." They want their money now. Wake up! It's time to go to work.

Finally, your ability to endure the building process is a tribute to your own dedication to your dream. While you are building your dream and waiting, don't let your *wait* become a *weight*. Keep believing! I started building on my dream in 1980, and it didn't become a reality until 1983. You have to keep the faith, stay focused, and keep building!

> While you are building your dream and waiting, don't let your wait become a weight.

Warring for Your Dream

Don't Quit!

When things go wrong as they sometimes will,
When the road you're trudging seems all uphill,
When the funds are low and the debts are high,
And you want to smile, but you have to sigh.
When care is pressing you down a bit –
Rest if you must, but don't you quit!

Life is queer with its twists and turns,
As every one of us sometimes learns,
And many a fellow turns about
When he might have won had he stuck it out.
**Don't give up though the pace seems slow –
You may succeed with another blow.**

Often the goal is nearer than
It seems to a faint and faltering man.
Often the struggler has given up
When he might have captured the victor's cup;
And he learned too late when the night came down,
How close he was to the golden crown.

Success is failure turned inside out –
The silver tint of the clouds of doubt.
And you never can tell how close you are,
It may be near when it seems afar.
**So stick to the fight when you're hardest hit,
It's when things seem worst that you mustn't quit!**

Author Unknown

CHAPTER 5

Warring for Your Dream

You can't kill my dream! You have to war for your dream. That means you have to do battle. You have to fight for your dream and not expect someone else to do all the fighting for your dream. Don't let someone else war for your dream more than you do.

Most people won't get behind you and support you and your dream if they don't see the fire of a warrior look in your eye! You have to have a warrior mentality. People must know that you are willing to fight and die for your dream.

> You have to have a warrior mentality. People must know that you are willing to fight and die for your dream.

I remember in the early stages of my business when things were really tough. The cash flow stopped flowing and business was real slow. It was during this time that my secretary said, "Why don't you give up before you get yourself so deep in debt and get yourself hurt?" I told her, "I can't give up now! I have come too far from where I started from. I'm in it too deep now. I have resigned my job and given up a steady paycheck for this dream. I have a retired and disabled mother who mortgaged her house for my dream. A single disabled woman invested her last $3 in my dream. My family and I have been living like paupers. I have made too many sacrifices to quit now. I will have to fortify myself, harden myself, strengthen myself."

You may have to fix your face like flint. Dig in for the long haul. I said to myself, "There are other people out there in this business who are making it, and the Bible says that God is not a respecter of persons. I'll just have to work smarter and harder."

> You may have to fix your face like flint. Dig in for the long haul.

You see, I had done my research and due diligence. I knew there was a need for my service in the Dallas metroplex. I also knew that the Dallas metroplex was home to many of the Fortune 500 companies. Plus, my business wasn't just a regional business. I was mailing for companies all over the country.

You have to do your research and make up your mind. You can't be double-minded in life. The power of a made-up mind is awesome! Many people never really make up their mind to do anything. *This means you completely devote yourself to your dream and you refuse to quit.*

> *Completely devote yourself to your dream and refuse to quit.*

I am committed to what I do. I am dedicated to what I do. I expect to win. Some people don't dedicate themselves to winning. I expect to win in everything I do in life. Once I make a commitment and devote myself to something, I will stay the course and see what the end will bring. You have to risk it all. I believe when life gets tough, you have to get tougher!

The Spirit of a Warrior

My mother imparted the spirit of a warrior in me. When she was pregnant with me, she had complications with her pregnancy and the doctor advised her to abort me, but she refused and made up her mind that she was going to war for her child.

I have been warring for my life all of my life. I will go into more detail about this in the Epilogue. Nothing comes easy in life. You have to war for whatever you want in life. I have been warring for everything in my life all of my life. I had to war just to get out of my mother's womb. I have been on my own since I was eighteen. I had to war my way through college.

On September 18, 1978, the Senior Vice President of Sales with FedEx called me into his office in Memphis and told me I had been given the job of Sales Rep with FedEx in Dallas. He told me, "Ray, you will be the first and only African-American Sales Rep with FedEx not only in Texas but throughout the entire Southwest." I asked him, "When do I report for duty, Sir?"

I welcomed the challenge, because I'm a warrior. I'm used to warring for things in life. Yes, it was a war, but I prevailed. I was recognized as the number one Sales Rep in our district several times. I won an all-expense paid trip to Hawaii for my sales performance.

Battle for Your Dream

When I started my mailing service, I found out that I was the first and only African-American commercial mailer in the Southwest. I had to do some warring, but in October 2002, I celebrated twenty years. You have to battle for your dream.

Don't let your dream die. War for your dream. Keep it alive. Never give up!

Personally, I have been tested physically, mentally, spiritually, and financially, but *I am a survivor!* You have to expect conflict, opposition, problems, obstacles, challenges, and struggles because they are coming whether you want them to or not. There are times your dream will cause you to be imprisoned. Martin Luther King, Jr.'s dream caused him to be in a physical prison. Your dream may cause you to be in a financial prison for a season, but

> Your dream may cause you to be in a financial prison for a season, but don't give up on your dream! Your breakthrough will come.

don't give up on your dream! Your breakthrough will come. In fact, it's on the way!

Sure, I have had many failures, setbacks, and disappointments along the way. So what? Life is a journey. It is a process. The shaping process takes a lot of time and it's got to be developed. Everything good takes time. But guess what? *The best is yet to come.* I don't know anyone who has lived for a while whose journey has always been easy and smooth. In life you will have hills and valleys, but keep working your dream.

When Times Get Tough, Get Tougher!

It wasn't easy starting and building my business, but it was worth it. You don't accomplish great things in life without a struggle. Remember, when times get tough, you have to get tougher. Nothing in life comes easy.

I have been fighting for my life ever since I was in my mother's womb. I'm a fighter. I want to win and I expect to win. Get back in the fight. Don't quit! I can't quit. I've got to have a survival mentality. I've got to have an "I'm going to make it" mentality. I have too much invested. My secretary told me one day to give up before I got hurt financially. She didn't realize I had too much invested in this thing. I had to keep warring and battling for my dream. You will have to battle for your dream too.

> Don't let your dream die. You have to nurture that dream, feed it, guard it, prune it, and speak to

Keep the dream alive. Don't let it die. Never give up! A life without risk is like no life at all. Hold fast to your dream. Fight for your dream.

Keep your dream alive. Don't let your dream die. You have to nurture that dream, feed it, guard it, prune it, and speak to it. But whatever you do, don't give up on your dream. Keep your dream alive. Don't let other people steal your dream or talk you out of it. Keep dreaming. Get it in your spirit. Get it in your soul.

Life is a war! Determine to fight for your dream until your dream has been fully achieved!

Teamwork Makes the Dream Work

"It takes a dream team to make BIG dreams come true."

Ray Orr

Teamwork Makes the Dream Work

Sometimes the dream is too big for one hero! Sometimes you will need help to build your dream. The bigger the dream, the more help you will need. I think most people's biggest mistake is trying to do everything by themselves. Even the Lone Ranger had Tonto to help him!

> I think most people's biggest mistake is trying to do everything by themselves. Even the Lone Ranger had Tonto to help him!

I don't know of any significant contribution that anyone has made to society and our universe who did it without some help. If you are going to build a house, you will need some help. If you are going to build a skyscraper, you will need even more help. The bigger the dream, the more help you will need. Rome was not built by one man. America was not built by one man. It takes teamwork. *Teamwork makes the dream work!* It will take teamwork to build your dream.

I had to get some investors and network my dream. You may need to do so too. Together, our dreams will become a reality. Zig Ziglar says, "You can get everything in life you want if you help enough other people get what they want."

Build Relationships

You will have to build relationships. Before I opened my mailing company, I met most of the mailers in the city and built a relationship with them. They gave me very valuable information. They told me how to quote jobs, schedule job production, utilize which vendors, and where to go for equipment and supplies. They told me of things to watch out for.

When I opened my business, the first customer I had was a mailing service colleague. I survived the first three months of business by handling all of the overflow work for the mailers I had built a relationship with. So whatever your dream is, start networking and building relationships with people who are already doing what you aspire to be doing. There will always be someone willing to help you if you have the right attitude.

Network

Network the dream. Stay in the network. You can overcome anything by working together.

You may need to solicit some help because sometimes the dream is too big for one hero. You may need to incorporate. I had to do that.

You have to constantly build relationships, relationships, relationships, and you have to network, network, network too!

Draw up a contract similar to the one that follows, sign it, and put it in a visible place where you see it every day.

Dream Contract

1. I will not let my dream die.
2. I will not let anyone kill my dream.
3. I will not let anyone steal my dream.
4. I will not let anyone burst my dream bubble.
5. I will fight for my dream.
6. I will pray for my dream daily.
7. I will work on my dream daily.
8. I will speak to my dream.
9. I will believe in my dream.
10. I will not quit on my dream.
11. I will not let my dream die.

I, _____, will work on my dream every day. I will fortify myself and fight for my dream. I will not let my dream die. I will realize my dream!

_____
Signature

_____
Date

Dream Like a Fool!

"The only impossible dream is the one you don't dream!"

Ray Orr

Dream Like a Fool!

*T*he only impossible dream is the one you don't dream! Dream like a fool! Dream beyond your means. You've got to dream beyond your means, because if you have the means, then there is no need to dream. You can just do it.

Keep dreaming! People may laugh at you, they may tell you it will never happen, but keep on dreaming. Look at the Wright brothers. They kept on dreaming. People told them that they were foolish and they never would build an airplane. But they kept on dreaming like fools. Thanks to them, we now fly all over the world.

Keep your dream alive. Don't let it die. You must nurture that dream, feed it, guard it, prune it, and speak to it. But whatever you do, don't give up on your dream. Keep it alive. Don't let other people steal your dream or talk you out of it. Keep dreaming. Get it in your spirit. Get it in your soul. It might be a pipe dream now, but keep on dreaming.

You may need to go and pick your dream back up! Someone told you that you were foolish to dream what you were dreaming. They told you it was impossible. Again, the only impossible dream is the one you don't dream. Pick your dream back up. It might be a Cinderella dream, but keep on dreaming. Cinderella's dream came true. It may be unprecedented, but keep dreaming like a fool.

People are not supposed to see it and understand it because it is your dream, not their dream. Keep dreaming like a fool. One day naysayers will be paying money to come see you or buy your products or services.

> Keep dreaming like a fool. One day naysayers will be paying money to come see you or buy your products or services.

Yes, dream like a fool! You may be incarcerated right now, but keep on dreaming. Keep on dreaming like a fool. Go ahead and dream the Cinderella dream. Go ahead and dream the impossible. *Dream because the only impossible dream is the one you don't dream.*

You may be homeless, or you may be on welfare, but keep dreaming like a fool! Go ahead and dream, baby! Dream like you don't have good sense. Dream like a fool. You may be seventy-five years old, but keep on dreaming because dreams fuel us and give us energy, inspiration, and motivation.

You may be on your sickbed, but keep dreaming. Dream about better days ahead. Dream like a fool!

Living Your Dream

"A man is what he dreams about all day long."

Ray Orr

Living Your Dream

Can dreams come true? Yes, dreams do come true! My dream came true, and yours can too!

A Dream and A Dollar is my story, and I believe it is your story too. It personifies and typifies most people's lives. It's a true story. It's a dream come true.

I remember working in the cotton fields of Mississippi and watching cars go by with luggage racks on the top. The people were going on vacation. I would dream about what it would be like to take a vacation. Go to nice places. Eat at a restaurant. Stay in a hotel. Ride in a nice car. I dreamed about having a family, a career, a nice house, and a nice car, just like the man on the front cover of this book.

When I finished high school in May 1971, I was eighteen and I had a wage earner job that summer. I saw guys we called "lifers" who worked at the plant until they retired. These lifers showed up to work every day just for the money. There was no satisfaction or fulfillment in what they were doing. I realized that summer that I didn't want to be a lifer and get stuck on a money job.

I enrolled in Memphis State University in the fall of 1971. In my senior year at Memphis State University, I got a part-time job working for FedEx. When I graduated from college in August 1978, I was offered a Sales Representative position with FedEx in Dallas, Texas. I had never flown before and I had never even been to Dallas, but I decided to take that leap of faith and relocate to Dallas as I mentioned in an earlier chapter. I learned early in life, "You have to follow the cheese!"

> The beauty about dreaming is that it is free. So why don't you "dream like a fool"?

I remember back in college at Memphis State University when some of my buddies and I would leave college and drive through Germantown, an affluent suburban area in Memphis. We would point at houses and say, "That is my house. That is my car." My favorite saying when I saw a house I liked was, "Ooo, I love this house!"

The beauty about dreaming is that it is free. It doesn't cost you a thing. You can dream about going to anyplace, living anyplace, and driving whatever you want to drive. It is absolutely free. So why don't you "dream like a fool"?

Don't Break Down! Break Through!

I traveled many rough and bumpy, dirty roads before I realized my dream. I have overcome tremendous odds all of my life. I decided I was not going to stay in my dream bubble and break down but break through! It is great to be out of that bubble. I'm a dreamer! I have always been full of big dreams. I'm no longer an anonymous dreamer, but now I'm a distinguished entrepreneur!

I had to go for it. My mother said, "Boy, that is a good job you have at FedEx and good jobs are hard to find." I said, "This isn't for me. I want to retire from my own company." I just had to do it because the cost of not fulfilling my dream was more than the cost of fulfilling my dream. You have to have that pining feeling to get out of your dream bubble.

I'm giving you the pin to use to burst your dream bubble and come out. I challenge you to come out of that bubble. Your future

Epilogue

is better than your past, and the best is yet to come. There is more ahead of you than what is behind you. There is so much more in you. You have to keep confessing that to yourself until you believe it. Don't get stuck in your past. Don't get stuck in your history. So what if you made some mistakes and bad choices? Who hasn't? The universe needs your dream to become a reality.

> Your future is better than your past, and the best is yet to come.

A Dream and A Dollar is the hallmark of my life. Hopefully, I have inspired and motivated you to dream or pick your dream back up. I'm a living witness that dreams do come true for plain, old, ordinary people like you and me. Remember, the only impossible dream is the one you don't dream. So go ahead and dream the Cinderella dream. I'm living my dream and it sure feels good!

Bibliography

Books:

Mary Kay Ash. *Mary Kay* (Harper & Row Publishers, Inc., 1981).

Robert A. Sigafoos and Roger R. Easson. *Absolutely Positively Overnight!* (Memphis, TN: St. Luke's Press, 1983).

Magazines:

Joan M. Feldman. "Federal Express: Making It Big with Small Packages," *Air Transport World,* July 1976.

Newspapers:

The Dallas Morning News, July 18, 2002.

Website Addresses:

www.marykay.com

www.mrsfields.com

www.thekingcenter.org/mlk/bio/html

www.oprah.com

www.abcnews.go.com/sections/business/dailynews/wendys thomas 020108html

www.findarticles.com/cf dis/m3191/19_110/63940956/p2articles.jhtml?term=

www.wendys.com

Visit us online at:
www.adreamandadollar.com and at
www.rayorr.com
Order online at:
www.adreamandadollar.com and at
www.wholearmourpublishing.com

For bookings contact:
Chris Howell
C&D ASSOCIATES
P.O. Box 300284
Arlington, TX 76007-0284
Office: 817-226-7296
Fax: 413-691-1896
email:chrihwll@aol.com

News
Articles
Book Club
Online Bookstore
Streaming Webcast
Chat Events
...And More

Epilogue

Life is a fight! I had to fight for my life from the time I was in my mother's womb. I had to fight just to get into the world, just to experience life, because my life was threatened and almost aborted before I got here.

I was born in 1953 in Marks, Mississippi, as the youngest of six children (all boys), born to sharecroppers Ella and Johnny Orr. My mother and father were separated. From the very beginning, my life was a battle. My birth almost cost my mother her life too. My mother and her five children were living with her sister and her husband in a four-room shack in Batesville, Mississippi. Now, sixteen people were living in a four-room shack with no indoor plumbing.

My mother went to the doctor in Batesville, and he told her that due to complications with her pregnancy, she would have to abort the baby. The options: She would die giving birth, or both of us could die during the delivery. My mother told the doctor that there was no way she would abort the baby. She would go through the delivery. She didn't have enough money to go to the hospital in Batesville, so she went to the Marks, Mississippi, hospital where I was born.

A year after my birth, my mother and family moved into a three-room shack. My family worked the blazing hot cotton fields of Mississippi, chopping and picking cotton from sunrise to sunset. We raised our own crops, which included okra, peas, greens, and corn, and we sold them to the market.

Even at a young age, I had a knack for business. I helped my mother establish a produce business from the back of the family's truck. My mother and I used to load up the truck full of products we had raised and went to surrounding cities and drove through the streets in the residential areas selling produce from the truck.

At the age of ten, I moved to Memphis, Tennessee, with my uncle and aunt. At the age of eighteen, after graduation, I got my own apartment, so I have been on my own since I was eighteen years old. I worked and paid my way through college and graduated from Memphis State University in August 1978 with a Bachelor of Business Administration Degree. I was the only one out of my family to finish high school and college.

Every person has a private dream, but without a strategy, prudent planning, management, and work (hard work), and perseverance, it will remain a dream and never become a reality.

Hopefully I have shared some strategies and given you some inspiration and motivation to help you solve the age-old problem of having *A Dream and A Dollar*. However, I would be remiss if I didn't tell you that some dreams come true and some don't. But keep on dreaming! Don't give up on your dream! You can make it! You can do it! You can be whatever you want to be, but you will never be any more than what you think you can be. You've got to dream!

Dream Notes

Dream Notes

Visit us online at:

www.adreamandadollar.com
and at www.rayorr.com

Order online at:

www.adreamandadollar.com
and at www.wholearmourpublishing.com

For bookings contact:

Chris Howell
C & D ASSOCIATES
P. O. Box 300284
Arlington, TX 76007-0284
FAX:413/691-1896
E-mail: chrihwll@aol.com

For graphic design and illustration contact:

David Wilson
ABC-Design
918/455-2097
E-mail: ddwilson@concentric.net

For text design contact:

Lisa Simpson
Words Unlimited
918/258-1330
E-mail: transcriberLS@cox.net

Dream Notes

Dream Notes

Dream Notes

Dream Notes

Dream Notes